Would You Be Made Whole?

Would You Be Made Whole?

sixty unruly sonnets

Gregg Friedberg

Kelsay Books

Cover photograph by Simon Messenger, Cumbria, UK

ISBN 13: 978-0692520277

Kelsay Books
Aldrich Press
24600 Mountain Ave 25
Hemet, California 92544

www.kelsaybooks.com

For Ken,
who bears with these obsessions unobsessively.

With thanks to Frank Bidart, Peg Boyers, Lee Gould, and other present and past participants in Frank's summer workshop at Skidmore College, to Nick and Jenny Barnes, and to Nancy Scott and Allan Popa for their encouragement and help with publishing these poems.

Acknowledgments

Poems in this book have previously appeared, some in different versions, in the following publications:

Daydreaming Magazine
Bride of Cyclops

Drexel On-line Journal
Agnus Dei

High Chair
In my ideal conception the lovers never speak

The Best Seat Not in the House
Notes toward a by mowing
Bathetic Fallacy

U.S. 1 Worksheets
After the party
Balustrade
Is that the monster Genghis Khan?
Of course I understand
This is no castle in Spain

Contents

Notes
About the Author

wayward eros   I

Of course I understand

                        and you've every right
to complain. Of course I've not forgotten:
I singled you out, conferred on you pride of place,
and now it's different, everything's changed.

Can't say why. Don't know myself—in either
sense of the phrase. Next season of life?
Eye for detail, gone blind? New creed, new drug,
new haircut—which are causes? which effects?

New people . . . can't be avoided. They fill
the old niches, it's true. Ersatz grandma
in the rocker—a surrogate baby for the crib!
And yes, your proxy to partner me in bed.

Of course I'm aware he's not you.
But under the circumstances he'll do.

Sirtaki

Why go up on the roof to dance, my
      partner's shoulder my sole retainer?

The edge fascinates, draws me like the flame
      the moth, and his gaze engaged rouses me.

So much romance I've a mind to die—
      fix the moment so it doesn't pall—else

we'll take the stairs down, he and I. No,
      I want to fly—of course *he* can: exalted

as angels, a laugh that takes wing. The edge
      moves in. Our kicks clear it—and then some.

Graduation not far-off now. No stately stride
      across the stage this time. Heel-toe sidle on

the very brink! He nods and winks: my trousers
      swell: the stars and the cars tilt and whirl.

Each morning first thing
I ask the half-light

"Why has he mistaken me?"
As my hand scans his side of the bed,
my mind scans that last little while
each night, last thing: he reads a book,
has enough, sets it down, switches off
the light, palm to chest reads me:
"You're fantastic," he whispers, "each day
more fantastic," . . . has enough, falls asleep,
leaves me to read myself, but *I* can't
get myself into focus. Each morning, *more*
of a blur: less substantial—more *phantasmal*—
soon a mirage in his empty bed, while he
brews coffee, starts his day downstairs.

Balustrade

A week into the renovation it had to be
removed. Then there was just the verge,
an eight-meter drop . . . seven if I landed
on the dining table. The risk, of course, of a false
move: precipitous step backward during
animated conversation, an absent one while
lost in thought . . . wee-hour confusion . . .

More worrisome, as it proved: the *beck*
of the unbuffered brink—stronger with each
transit of the landing. Resisting the impulse to leap
made me dizzy, and you suspected, erected
a makeshift barrier, reduced my sense of the thing
to the ordinary . . . like your embrace when we
climbed Vulcano, stood at the rim of its crater.

After sex you say you're into me

but doubt I'm into you. I resist pointing
out the obvious, reply, "But I'm into *this*:
that I have the power to deprave you,
from a poised guy self-possessed to one
beside himself, obsessed. At my short order,
you turn abject predator, I imperious prey.
Yes, I scry the faults of your plaster sky,
but it's your failed control in my mind's eye:
how your frantic tongue prefers, to deluxe
delicacies, even what of me's least savory,
how *beyond* your might you strive to sow
your second selves in my sterile ground,
how spent, bewildered, you thank me . . .
you're welcome."

In my ideal conception

the lovers never speak.
I contrive every manner of impediment:

corner them oppositely in crowded,
cacophonous rooms, blaring public squares,
hushed theater boxes, hurry them separately on.

Tie their tongues when finally they meet.
Allow them only the conversation of the senses:
it makes no claim of truth beyond itself.

Its ways are the process of the earth
but writ intimately: upheavals, scrapes
and shudders, hot flows, the ticklish precession
of the poles—their thrilling reversal,

and as with the hurricane's eye,
just the tease of a lash renews the fray.

If after a night of fitful sleep

                                        the room
you wake up in's mostly strange (as if
you'd spent a night here just once before,
too long ago to place), then you throw off
the covers, rise and explore: each thing
you inspect fascinates. Over the mantle
a portrait: no dandified forebear—a panda!
In those wide, glistening eyes you recognize
you've found and lost yourself before.
On the desk a note. Of its light-fantastic hand
you sense the potential in yours. Addressed
to the boy you laid siege to in sixth grade?
You realize with a start: to the man
softly snoring on the unfazed side of the bed.

Notes toward a Boy Mowing

My hand's teaching you, shuttling slowly
below the sill, about the boy mowing
the common, breaking the Sabbath.

He's carved clumsy initials on the bases
of birches, sparks a knob of granite now
and again. Woke the dog, then seduced her!

To the lord of the land complain,
to the tablets and gavel of village council!

Vainglory his standing blue veins. Go down,
stand in his way, peep into his shirt, into
the shimmery vale of sweat,

wag your finger: *mustn't pet her*
Every one of his fingers a mischief . . .
and the salt licks of his golden calves.

Double Jeopardy

An all-out sprint, then three days on the couch,
        hobbled, whining, wanting service.
Sworn innocent, but sneak peruser of *Martyrs
        Magazine*. Poet's muse but with only
passing interest in these lines—not Narcissus,
        neither connoisseur. Brilliant,
sometimes, his jests ad lib. Mostly ennuyant.

But one day—imminent, I dread—will spell black
        alchemy, turn his native gold to lead.
He'll hole up in an oubliette, and cuffed to a rank
        wall, beg lashes of his thuggish guard,
then solace in those arms. And so unboyed—and
        I unmused—he'll slip a hand up
through the grate and wave, supposing me amused.

Do you recall?

We'd made love on a butte:
you on your back, gazing up at the moon—
honey and harvest—I on my haunches,
still inside you. "Sublime!" you said,
and then, "Please: don't leave me behind."

I thought you meant me. It's been three days
since the catastrophe, since the rival planet
trawled by, trolled it away—you with it.
No hole in the sky, exactly.

The sky's not empty, for sure it's not. But
it's all so remote, nothing near. And no tide—
not at sea, not in me—all ebb, no swell!
I think: "Go ahead, tidy up, have a sandwich."
Then I recall. Then I've no will left at all.

The Boy Rapunzel

From your high keep survey the expanse
that's all your world and not at all your world.

Pygmies hoe the radish rows, herd short-horned voles
over the horizon where, you suppose,

the grass is greener. This morning you awakened
to a disemboweled princeling bobbing

from your hair, your warder's squeals of savage glee.
You're the bait of choice—against your will,

of course. Tiptoe around your stony cell, prime your
arches, contemplate the leap: desperate resort before

another randy noble boy falls victim. In a dug-out
beetle, set on the window sill just so, brew ink,

indite laments: imagine that your penis or your pen is
mightier than your warder's terrible slow sword.

His hand clasps yours
like a crab its prey

Are you loved or merely abducted?

The rearview mirror's crazed like God's creation,
        devours the present, voids it as past—

the back gate of Eden. Nothing blessed but to be
        damned. A trompe-l'oeil cornucopia.

Love just now, though, isn't it? Bask
        in the blissful moment, on the doddery,

raggedy seat, shimmy past the gleaming wolf packs.
        Lo! an inviting sign: "Rogue Outfitters"

Are you low on anything? Reach for the Nutella
        beneath the seat, check your level.

Show the boy at the wheel. The old Chevy winks,
        slows, veers onto the exit ramp, under
                the no-fault sky.

ars poetica **II**

I once knew a boy

                          —very sure of himself—
who claimed that Truth was the show playing
in the chrome bumper of his old Chevy.

He'd sit for hours, entranced by the fun-house
swells and bends, flares and glares—
sporadic flourishes or frenetic stabs of his pencil.

He disapproved of regular syntax, rejected
its crude assertiveness.
                          I'd sit beside him,
try to fathom the rust-pocked phantasmagoria,
looked to the poem growing in his lap for clues.

But for me what was true was him, his lank,
hairy thighs through the rips in his jeans. His
trances occasioned my own.
                          What stopped me
slipping a finger through, sampling the truth there,
was different from what stopped him slipping
through the chrome.

The poet (like God)

                                's not boxed in prim
boxes, ashamed of a fart, proud of his smarts
(or contrariwise). He's out in the current
that's wholly spirit, fishing with lures
like a Grecian urn or a Tennessee jar,
and he doesn't just go with the flow: where
there's pure receptivity there's total control.

Flush with what words can never do justice
to he makes do: becomes Jesus and mixes
with lay men and women, spells out a parable,
works a cool miracle, milks an ocean of sap
from the tit of an aphid, never (like Him)
frustrated: from the wreckage of Babel
he launches balloons of hot prayer.

Poets' Workshop

Might I make a delicate (indelicate?) request?
This summer while we're here together, I'd like
to copulate with one—or several—of you.

I guess I've always believed—since the tenderest
of the post-tender years (instinct pure?)—
that a person might know another (I mean *really*
know) only when there's carnal knowledge too.

You beg to differ. Even object rudely! Urge
a veritable Everest of exceptions:
next of kin, kindred spirits—declare them not
exceptions at all but proof to the contrary!

I'm sorry, I can't help it. You'll not change
my mind. So please indulge me? grant me
the chance, *without* words, to change (transfigure?)
yours.

Esprit

Should it focus there, it might coax bananas
from arctic February, lure parrots to Baffin
Bay though birds borealis they never were!
It's—I've guessed, haven't I?—the hero of that
book you're writing, in sheer disguise.

Yet it has girlish grace, and though it be
d'un certain âge. A parodist's sense of humor,
refractory giggle. Deft mime of your old
flame, *de feu mon prince,* our far offspring.

It's been reproached: for both exaggeration
and insufficiency, as through a glass convex
or darkly. But the truth, I think, is: it *fore*tells,
don't you? Or when it (then we call it love)
bedazzles: blissful blear until the sear spots clear.

The Sonnetoid Manifesto

Are the cars disordered? not locomotive,
first class, second, then caboose. And are
the stations? unscheduled stops, scheduled
ones sped through . . . who would want to be
conveyed so? A tragic train-wreck of a sonnet!

But let go that conceit: what if it model
the paradigm of *all* human conceit? riff
the rough genius of English? (on a ground
of Grendel's grunts, Virgil's grandeur!)

One hundred forty syllables (give or take
a few) arrayed in fourteen (like-length?) lines,
in order agonized—or with ecstatic grace!—
honed to one fine point: an essay's single
sharpest claw cleaned of the limerick's cloy.

He's my friend, he claims,

                          misses
no occasion to expose my foibles.
Draws me out on the limb of my vanity . . .

I wonder that he bothers: left to my own
devices, I embarrass myself.

Publish photos of myself nude.
Under my own name. Unveiled face.
Nothing to be ashamed of, right?

And, of course, there are the poems.
But concerning them I've been told:
"A tease of veils. Better drop them."

Once a month I read in public.
If I read in the raw would I write rawer?
My friend never fails to attend.

A Dare

Sooner or later, he told me, you'll write
      a poem about a door.
Because a door's a prime confusion: dam
      and sluice, sexton *and* midwife.
When there's no difference between the out
      and the in, nothing discrete
nor indiscreet, then a door gives a false
      impression. Likewise
the wall it breaches, and the room. There
      are none of these in heaven.
Neither in hell. The realm of doors, of hide
      and seek, strut and coy
is here and now. I dare you, he said, write
      the poem about a door.

alter egos III

After the Party

The boy unbuttoning, shrugging off his shirt,
getting ready for your bed is only your
lamplight shadow. The hands at your belt
buckle are only yours.
                                In your mind's eye
and ear: the sultry dancing, frothy fawning,
a stubbled throat, larynx flirting . . .
                                        between
his pantcuff and slouched sock nakedness
you couldn't stop your eye returning to—
a boy, like you . . .
                        why do you burn to possess
your double? You were sure you'd betray
yourself if you stayed longer.
                                Now you're
free to stare, stroke that exposé of leg,
slide your fingers up the pantleg to
the mounded calf, have your way with him.

Wraith

If you approach this corner as if on felt
at the hour when your shadow vanishes,
cross your arms, chin to chest, so it appears
you're nodding off or not yourself, eye
askant the dappled bench where afternoons
you fell asleep, book to breast, find and fix
the oblique line of sight that reveals
a panorama not of deserted space
but of all your novice hours in this place,
then into your eye corner we'll crowd—
boys and youths you were—settle long enough
to tie a lace, count coins, recover breath . . .
So unsuspecting, smooth our hands and face,
you're tempted to look up and stare.

My friend wears too much make-up

I've never seen her *un*besmirched, can't help
but think: *clown*. I took a poll: 98
out of 100 mutual friends share my distaste.

The other 2? They just like to be *outré*.
(They're like that.) Even so, I suspect
all of us judging judge confined
to some cramped chamber of the mind,
                                 strict-ruled cell.
Whereas she considers from her storied
vantage, private panorama composed
not alone of form and color but of seasons,
all their vagaries, her soul's expanse . . .
                                 each morning
as she stands before her mirror, wielding
the tube of rouge, that nostalgist's finger.

This is no castle in Spain

not even a tearoom on the Cornish coast.

No, you can't watch through the portcullis
crusader knights fly kites, nor from the windowed
bay pirates under gingham sails.

A flirty fire in the corner, but not because
it's Christmas. It's just to cozy this interlude
of drizzle before the long, clear evening.

On the porch a paper boy is sheltering.

He'll catch the wind, swoop around in a quirky
way, pancake bottom up. Yes, I know about boys:
wisecracks, pranks, no truck with misery.

In this interlude, his ordinary boyhood,
are there moments when you let yourself breathe
easy, you who love him? A breath or two?

Snow Globe

Just stepped inside, a break from shoveling
snow, heaping it beneath the ice-floed windows,
tassel-capped like my double inside
the crystal ball he's peering into,
the last of the confetti settling. He looks up,
confirms I'm watching, relaunches it.

Long since he dubbed the one boy me. Himself
my friend. Then their frozen play seemed too
constrained to envy. But now he's thinking
how simply, in their glass orb, love's refreshed.
He glances at my frosty boots. His shoulders
want my *un*gloved hands—across the room.

Propose southern climes? He knows as well
as I the faded light's not due to latitude.

"Yankee Mortified near New Florence"

Having gleaned a fleshy ear of corn
in the dining car of the Columbus
& New Haven, Limited,
     disclosed
to himself in the window a panoply
of yellows imbricate, tooth
      and kernel,
he suffered the familiar pang:
dignified by the exquisite function
of his intellect, humbled by the licit
function of his flesh . . .
      reflected—
while picking clean the pulpy crevices—
how art that's more than artifice discloses . . .
does not quite disclose . . .
      considered
how seldom he felt August as he used to . . .
mostly, remembered how he used to.

My neighbor's smoke rings

                                             are the present
proxy for my self-disgust, his ashtray
its emblem, his wheezing its motto.

I imagine him shooting flying squirrels,
disgust myself further: I, curator
of clay pigeons. He's the enduring bronze
and I, the lost wax.
                                       He passes me
a recording of himself and his bald mistress
rutting by the fixed flicker of fake logs.
As ardently consensual as molten metal
and the waiting mould.
                                   I nod acknowledgment,
hand back to him the grunting gadget,
with sly fingers pencil epitaphs like
"A man who had better never been."

Contagion

I see myself reflected in a tear—
    in sorry haste thumb it off his cheek—
pure sympathy distilled of *my* distress:
      he found me down and himself powerless

to pick me up—a failure without precedent.
    Til now his absence ended was enough
to replenish my joy in full and at
      no cost to him of strategy or toil.

Does this drug too lose its potency
    like base fixes do? Not *true* magic
so once regarded skeptically, then dis-
      credited—like rabbits' feet and Lourdes?

I had the robust health of his charmed place.
    Now he too is ailing in my blighted space.

I too have been absent

                              failed a boy myself.

It was when this boy was sick, in a sick room,
a sick bed. On the pillow beside his was no
impression of my head.
                    When he came to
he asked for me. What's to say? I had a cold
so stayed away. A cold's the last thing you want
to give a boy with a broken skull, sneezing's
the last thing he'll like to do.
                          That was all true.
I told myself no lie. It's what I didn't tell:
that the sea's become oblivion again, that
every myth, including love has died.

After three days his father said, *he's dead*—
                              meaning me.
Might as well be, he mumbled.
Dead, he told this boy. Might as well be.

(un)redeemed IV

Agnus Dei

I do, my love, hear your pathetic stifled
bleats, the muted tinkle of your snow-packed
bell. I see: once again you're buried
in a drift—puny ridge that brawny brutes
stride through. I feel, though distant,
what no one nearer feels: your fear. Up to me,
if saved you shall be, to sound the alarm.

But don't *you* feel each next rescue less as
relief than pregnant with your next and worse
predicament? which wouldn't you be spared
this time, my love? (though it be hard:
a brief while longer full of fear), this time
prefer I stay my hand? stay still
while your shivers and little cries die down.

Pietà

It's in the grotesque that's made manifest
the *very* mind of God. Though not all that's
weird is sacred: there's the flare in God's eye
but also the glare. The trick is telling
them apart.
           May I tell you something
always yearned for, never confessed?
From that tenderest age when first I learned
of her, I've envied Mary . . . wanted to be her,
want the Annunciation made to me—yes,
and all that must ensue.
                Don't scowl—
it *was* a miracle, wasn't it?
and on miracles there's no need to stint!
I've never aspired to *be* our Lord,
always to suckle, then to pity Him.

52

"Take Me," He Said

I took him in my arms. His breath reeked
of death. I thought of his poor mother, death
kicking inside her. So keen was he to redeem,
he slipped the devil my card, conjured the romance
of the brink, swore, "I'll catch you," flexed
his biceps, flaunted the skull and crossed bones.

He was the genius of the cracking cornice
I strolled below, the snarling cur I fell before,
the aghast mask that's become my face.
he put things deftly into place just so they
might decay, arranged them to go awry.
"Take me," he said. "Sweep the stakes of Heaven."

Knowing him was more daunting, even,
than knowing nothing at all.

Stunt double

In a doorway, in shadow, silent, I watch
his halting, hard ascent. My feet aren't
raw, nor my shoulders sprained. My
unstubbled face doesn't bleed, sweat, and tear.

He draws on a last reserve of will, staggers,
falls, and fallen, pants beneath his cross
with the dregs of strength.
                                        My body
doesn't quiver. When I shrug and roll
a shoulder, then the other and massage it,
he crooks an arm, clenches a fist so
the biceps shudders, mounds and shivers.

When I mime heaving something heavy,
heavy, cast it off, he hoists, reshoulders it,
drinks from my dismay, rises, staggers on.

Ravaged and exposed,
are you also beautiful?

Not in the eyes of those who jeer you, those who
grieve, but in a buffered square on this gallery
wall. Here God's martyred blessed are delicacies.

By means of your excruciation He's cancelled sin,
annulled despair. I've fixed that fixing moment.
Now your staked foot is dressed with a blue ribbon.

I speak of you familiarly, how you acquiesced
in your portrait, then in the shift of your 'scene'
to mine where raw distress is not patent in the sun,

where God's love has scarcely any heat, barely
penetrates, and rings cliché. When they
take you down, you'll lie awhile on your mother's

lap, beneath high vaults, in grand salons.

Is that death in your lap?

or just a boy dead to the world?
The irregular holes in his palms, in his soles,
the rosy ring of pricks around his skull—are they clues?

The gash in his side, is it real? Try it.
Each fingertip makes its own memories, bears
its own witness . . . surmises, adores, regrets. Taste it.

At moments like this receiving's as blessed
as giving. The two ways of betting.

Did you know all along?—expect the sad mess
in your lap? *Ever* breathe easy? Count those moments
on the fingers of one of his hurt hands.

If you embrace a boy in his coltish time, in his time
of play and pleased sighs, does that oblige you later?

What if you've not got the stomach for it?

Gospel

I was his follower, *wasn't* I?
*Im*pure of heart, pretended fealty, but, really,
envious of his charisma, jealous of his
favorites . . . craved his sway *and* his love.
Neither could, nor can, be mine, but now
it's mine to fashion or efface his reputation.

Glorious? Or deluded the career that led
to that gruesome fate meted pretenders
to the hocus-pocus throne. The verdict rests
with my conflicted pencil—whether, even,
to put it to paper. Let him fade from unprompted
memory?—avenge myself so? Or let it tell?

Which words, then, the last to stir his earthly
lips? Will he have died forgiving or forsaken?

And this is the garden

                       where he suffered.
It smells of hurt and trouble, doesn't show
well, what with the bolting weeds, the curing dung,
the bloodied props lying where he shed them,
the shaggy spider flourishing behind the sepulcher.

The place has worn a veil of sorrow since
his close attentions turned to visions, since
he roamed and maybe died. Remember how
it tried his patience? how this ground teemed
with cunning, creatures cursed with cunning?—

in the shadows, seers who read true
religion into his thick quiet, his least
fidget or tic. Now there's just his breath
in the grass, breaking on the chinked wall.

Bathetic Fallacy

It's the jig's-up sun betrays you: simple shiner
with no discretion. Who would have thought
dumb constancy would be deemed love?

That's the poet's part in it—preposterous
minstrel, tipsy in jingle-bell slippers,
fast and loose with equations.

The litter and the lizard bask in the blind largesse,
wink now and again at a quivering meal
in its betrayed hiding place.

Was it a wild quip I let slip misled you,
led you to expect the music of the spheres
and not double-cross accounting?

love but not a muffled scream for it beneath
quaked ruins? not a red-faced itch below the belt?

Gone Too Far. Too Far Gone.

Not so long ago—I'm sure you recall—
I was in the thick of things, bull's eye
for God's slings and arrows, validated by

a March hare's leer. But then I took it
all wrong. Without the grain of salt. Snide asides
to the audience. Off-the-cuff plays for sympathy.

Odd-man-out I've proved to be, a threat
to the scheme of things—this bawdy house,
huckster's mall. I subvert its disintegrity.

Mine will be a subtle kind of exile: still lit
by the equal-opportunity sun, now and again
a dustmote's careless bed. Some twig may yet

yield to my hand or fly give me berth. But *he*
won't be noticing me. He's closed the book on me.

To a Wasp Dead on a Sill

                              All your care
was to probe the pane, lap its bright promise,
craving the gap that would yield it. Over
and over I took the pulse of your heart's
blind lunge, prayed the tide of rust blood
would flood high enough, flush you out
of the frame, through the wide, open door.

If I'd seized your wings? dragged you free?
You'd have stung me. Or destroyed yourself
resisting. *What does* he *want?* you thought,
something for himself? Why did you never think:
something for you. Over and over I signed
to you, *follow me*, went and came to show
you the ease that trivialized your trial utterly.

Yule

The sickest sun has died in naked woods
behind a curing shed. Woodfirelit, above
the bed, glass eyes in antlered heads flicker:

cordial, alert. Christ's cross-contorted face
gleams, transfigures, anticipates his birth.
Yours winces, against mine hard pressed.

"Would you be made whole?" inquires
the tenor. The chorus clamors for an answer,
falls silent. Stark, our gasps and groans.

Suddenly the cellos surge, crest, shudder
to a basal thrum, recover in a distant key.
Beneath the gallery of sly or blazoned injuries,

we lie feverbroken, raw, indecorously panting,
maculately healed.

Edgy Options

Carnal house, carnival, circus, cabaret—
arenas, roosts of rogue repute, catering
for those spells of raw appetite that afflict
even the prop'rest Victorian gentlemen,
the primm'st ladies,
                             home to freaks, foreskin
fanciers, where stuffed shirts meet bare bosoms,
the minuet devolves to bumps and grinds . . .

Shift your aim: from distant Utopia
                             to close sleight-of-hand.

Bask in the tricked applause, the duped cheers.
Never hit the sack but there's a mime on your back.

And should the excitement flag, the greasepaint
and glitter one day fail to convince, the remedy's
always at hand: just swallow the sword to the hilt,

        or let my smirk be your trapeze.

Far ago and long away

my tie was cinched
awfully *awfully* tight. I hung in the moonlight.

In my woozy sight a lantern swung. The watch-
man cut me down, bared my teeth and gums,
depressed my tongue, breathed me back . . .
to 'life'?
"Are you versed," he asked as soon
as it made sense, "in aubergine cuisine?"
"Only unsavory verse," I gasped. "Tell me
where I am?"
"Where you've always longed to be,
and when—though've never been. Where sirens
croon, bad seeds don't sprout. Where tedium
is done without.
Sieve the dunes between your toes.
Forget the trouble nobody knows you've seen.
Breathe easy—you've got your grace period."

mysteries, inside & out V

Is that the monster

                                    Genghis Khan
struggling with his cane and the front door?
Should I shove it closed against him? or help
because now he's past doing harm, his feeble
body more than he can manage.
                                    Madonna's
on the wall above the plate rail, immaculate as
ever, so you might think his Reign of Terror
was weathered without lasting harm.
                                    Might, but don't.
Even so, have pity? ease him onto the counter stool
like when he was a wee lad. Who could have
guessed the trouble he'd cause?
                                    It seems he's glad
to be here, regressed to innocence. Likes the pie,
that's clear, chin hung with glaze. I've a mind
to be, but won't be, stingy with the napkins.

Yes, there's the level playing field

But there's also the stacked deck.

Two kinds of fun,
dollhouse and dungeon.

If I'm too prissy, then the gamy world
of naughtiness is closed to me.

All the groovy things
goody-goody you won't do!

Add a pinch of victimhood to my relations,
predator sometimes, sometimes prey.

Cruelty's the salt
in the porridge of kindness.

Even execution has a flipside: all attention's
sexy if you let it be.

A matter of attitude adjustment,
to a very great degree.

"La mayoría de la gente prefiere tener razón que ser feliz"

So reads the banner beneath this mural.
The image has decayed beyond ken—
I *think* I see demons.
      We're taught:
to be right is, if not happiness per se,
then its sine qua non. As concerns
creature comfort, likely so. But beyond
that mere minimum?
      The proverb implies
the two are antitheses—isn't that queer?
To be human *and* happy requires we
suspend disbelief not just at the theater!

Reject the clinician's assessment our latest
amour's a treatable hormone imbalance.
Ignore the apostate boors who impugn
as fraud our deathbed dalliance with God.

Loss

once it's in the mind nesting
with the thing lost, recurs . . . recurs and recurs.
This is a grand feature of the mind.

Here's another:
you can lose what you've never had.
The imagined lost—the wished but unattainable—
makes in the mind just as sick a bed.

At first, to be sure, there's some difference
in quality. But with time and rehearsal
the difference disappears:

The 'real' loses a little reality.
The merely imagined gains some.

With time then—time that's called 'healing'—
comes a kind of mediocrity: *the habit of grief.*

Far Fetch

Richer experience of life than mine
     in ways: rarer smells, shriller noise, far less
squeamish, eagerer to serve.
                    And yet—
     I hate to say—a vast and influential
firmament is perfectly beyond his ken:
     stocks and credits, ancient Egypt, holy war,
Planck's constant . . . Proust's madeleine?

     Ignorant of all that teeming past and
presence, yet, it seems, not bewildered—
     often blissful!—seldom at a loss or at
wit's end, sizing, down his canine nose,
     things up.
               But I'm uneasy, often sore,
regarding the Big Picture I suspect I'm in,
     can't step back from, out of for a look.

It seems I'm always after

what proves to be a little off,

the sort of thing I've been known to call
a sure thing, or frantically to pray for.

So I've taken to looking through him, asquint
or askew, and setting my mind to jitterbug.

Not scattered, no. Focused but without dibs.
There, I've said it: "without dibs"

—that's the smart view. Now he's sharp
as a hamster running a wheel, the very picture

of head-down sympathy. Through the fence
slats, the cage bars, the black veil, I can't

make him out unless I focus on *anything* else.
Else it's crumbs he tosses me—or starves me blind.

Any commitment is a failure

of imagination. Seeing it through, the act
of a coward. Foolish, foolish consistency.

I'm permitted entry into the Great Treasury
and what catches my eye? Not the cataracts
of baubles, the flickering stereopticons,

but a chit on the checkered floor.

Captivates my sense of possibility, and I
hustle over to it, snatch it up, possess it
like it were Olympic Gold!

Why has God wasted Creation on the likes of me?

One of the questions on my roster of queries
of God. Really all the same one, all variations
on my abject theme.
                    Why do I ask?

This afternoon I crawled inland

                 paused now and again to read
the litter's semaphore, happened upon a shambly
establishment scarcely anchored to the grit.
Inside: a boy perched on a tripod over a foul pit.

He was in a tormented trance—squirmed, grunted,
wailed—which induced in me no little excitement:
finally, the prospect of an answer.
                            "Where to crop?"
I asked him, gesturing at the various infinities
outside the shack, "and what's the proper frame?
the right scale and resolution?" Of course,
I had in mind the very picture of contentment.

He shrieked—shrieked again, then issued from him
a voice surely not his own:

    "Ima make you a pancake, sugah,
    'n' drown it in Jemmy's own sweet sauce!"

No eyes atop my head

No insight into the depths beneath my feet.

He's just trickled molasses above my cage
onto my head. I jump—hiss! He reaches in,
swabs me with a finger. *Lick it.*

I do, but sulkily. He offers his palm. *Climb aboard.*
Sets me down beside his foot sinister.
I stare at the great toe. My revenge.

As if to say, the rest of him's not so great.
Come on, then. He hands me back into the cage,
and I make for my desk. I've been writing:

a long, discursive piece on the states of existence,
the spectrum from pure matter to pure myth,
from being merely a thing to being merely meaning.
                              He leaves me to it.

I watch as he prepares our morning coffee

pours himself a mug, me a thimble,
slips it into the holder just
inside my cage door, sits down beside.

We sip, collect ourselves, suppose how those selves
might fare through the course of the new day:
solve the world's problems, fast-followed by our own.

Of less ambitious projects, likelier accomplished,
he floats the prospectus: shopping, baking
(he has a sweet tooth!), a little tidying, grooming—

our domiciles and 'persons' . . . poetasting . . .
no fixed order—as the spirit moves us along!

I climb the wire mesh, peer out from loftier
vantage briefly, descend, sip, mount my wheel.

Le Bel Aujourd'hui

It shall make my friend nervous, I think, if I
start every day dancing.

                           We've made a pie
from the Apple Tree–it's not been denatured
chemically. The fruit's plagued: blotched and
pocked.

               That's not the worst of it! We pared *that*
away, and the rest, baked in the pie, is grubby
and glazy.

               He's sealing a Dark Room in the cellar,
toxic chemistry inside. Let there be . . . Magic!
Black and White.

                     But do you think he'll stay
with it? Or just shave the Evil Radish to pay for
all the apparatus?

                 Do you think he'll stay with me?
Don't tell him I asked! He sends the usual
mercurial greetings.

                   You see, I might have started
out this way: the Matador's funeral was yesterday.

Bride of Cyclops

I'd broken a pose, come out of the trance,
and there he was, observing through his monocle.

He set a mug between us: "Share?" Then asked:
"What's wrong?"

> *Tea* and *sympathy?*
> *—don't let's get your hopes up.*

How to explain? How even to start? I began
   to hyperventilate.

Everything's bone gray, it occurred to me to say.

> *Or blood red.*

Instead I laced my fingers atop my head, let
my elbows hang down like a veil hiding an eye.

> *Bride of Cyclops.*

"Claim me," I said and found his eye with mine.
"Install me on your grounds, in your bed."

> *Keep you distracted.*

"There's someone for everyone," I said. "Please."

A corsair's life

                         is fraught with perils,
unsympathetic encounters, so he'll
be after the matedness that nerves, that restores
the zest to derring-do. Not woe-is-us keening
between I've-got-your-back naps.

Have you chosen wrong your whole life long?

Boys want playmates, not mopemates,
so he returned to the sea without me.
He was sorry, recognized my good qualities:
tacky lips, tight ass.
                         But all is not, perhaps, lost.
He'll put in again for a visit. And meanwhile
I'll reform: live each day so it's someone
else's last, and each night as if it were mine.

Have you chosen wrong your whole life long?

I've taken to hopping about of late

Suits me. Better than ambling. And I do
less with my hands, keep them tucked at my sides,
more with my head—a real gain in the sense

of immediacy: my nose in lots of business
always before I'd been too squeamish
to explore. Headaches at first, but they passed.

What persists is a much diminished appetite
for opinions—I mean, concerning matters
remote from my here and now. I'm convinced,
my sphere of *real* influence has grown.

I keep an eye out for drones, stand-your-ground
enthusiasts. I suppose, under mortal threat,
I'd leap into a thicket, keep still. Not drop
to my knees. Dial 9-1-1. Speak in tongues.

Binocular

In clefts of calcite cliffs that seemed at first
dun sky thirteen black lozenges—what are they,
arrowhead-arrayed? I raise my spyglass . . .

They're nesting eremites in swarthy sackcloth!
Unmoving, self-confined to crusty aeries.
Unmoved, seers past earthly into azury

mirages. Ah! buzzard pairs—chick-bereft
to madness?—feed them! Do worming
coprophages preen them? But look!

A springyspray of creamgreen toads descends,
in glistening drool bewebbing them and them-
amidst a blondbright youth. Lithefingers he

his spangled flute and evileyes—I shift
my glass—the suburb on the facing rise.

I crave and crave that vantage

                                    that costs
my very self: unselfseeking being
in the world. *Had* I that sense of being—
want then become pure wonder—I
would not be I. And though it would transcend
all dread once accomplished, such self-
divestiture I dread. So I remain:
prisoner-servant of that petty tyrant Ego,
bide diseased time—my face each hour
its longer register, and strung between
those remote poles of all and none I swing
bewildered, pay out, reel in my tedious
contradiction. I know full well, cannot
accept: there is no *human* soul in paradise.

The Plexiglas peak

                              deployed on each
table with salt, pepper, sugar, napkin
holder announces the specialty of the house.

Same every day, though "fresh every day":
trout with clarified butter or with cilantro
jelly. Or "a la Veracruzana".

I wonder how that translates on the plate.
Met a sailor there . . . in port for a couple
of days—what's *that* got to do with it?

Can't say. I understand nothing. Used
to think it necessary to understand. It's not.
Thought it important, at least. Not so.

That the unexamined life's not worth
living. It just might *be*. I bet it is.

Notes

"Would You Be Made Whole?": from the New Testament, John 5 –
The Healing at the Pool: Jesus inquires of a man, for very many years
an invalid, if he would be healed.

"Sirtaki": a Greek line dance, known also as "Zorba's Dance" since
being 'featured' in the film *Zorba the Greek*.

"Agnus Dei": 'Lamb of God', a title for Jesus, especially in his role as
the universal sacrifice.

"Yankee Mortified near New Florence": as if the headline of a news
article. After Wallace Stevens' "Anglais Mort à Florence."

"La mayoría de la gente prefiere tener razón que ser feliz": In English:
"Most people prefer to be right than to be happy."

"Le Bel Aujourd'hui": title taken from one of the most admired
lines in modern French poetry, the opening of Stéphane Mallarmé's
sonnet "Le Cygne" (The Swan): "Le vierge, le vivace, et le bel
aujourd'hui . . ."— the elegant exuberance of which defies
translation, but here's a pedestrian version: "The virgin, the lively,
the lovely today . . ."

About the Author

Gregg Friedberg grew up in Columbus, Ohio, but for many years has lived in Upper Sandusky, a rural county seat, and nowadays spends half of each year in Guanajuato, Mexico where he participates in the bilingual arts-and-culture scene and gives regular readings.

Professionally he's been a partner in a computer software company, writing applications for Ohio county government, but has always written poetry, is happiest when writing sustained sequences, loosely but not conventionally narrative, treating a matrix of themes from an evolving perspective.

An example is *The Best Seat Not in the House* (Main Street Rag, 2010) which examines the vexed relationship between Creator and creature, whether God and man or author and protagonist.

In *What's Wrong*, a longer sequence, the first-person narrator is a refugee from American marketing culture.

Friedberg is completing a collection of photographs with corresponding texts, *The Artist's Reception*, the result of the black-and-white figure photography project he's been working on the past several years. The texts, which also tell a story, incorporate some of the wittier comments that have been posted with the photos at the art site deviantart.com. Excerpts have appeared in the art magazines, *Noisy Rain* and *Vitruvian Lens*.

And for the past ten years Friedberg has been a member of Frank Bidart's summer workshop at Skidmore College.

gefriedberg@gmail.com